Waiting for Saint Brendan
and Other Poems

DAVID McLOGHLIN

salmonpoetry

Published in 2012 by
Salmon Poetry
Cliffs of Moher, County Clare, Ireland
Website: www.salmonpoetry.com
Email: info@salmonpoetry.com

ISBN 978-1-908836-05-2

COVER ARTWORK:
Harry Clarke RHA, (1889-1931), *The Meeting of St Brendan with the Unhappy Judas*, Stained glass, 66.7 x 51.4 cm, Crawford Art Gallery, Cork, photography by Dara McGrath
COVER DESIGN: *Siobhán Hutson*

Salmon Poetry receives financial support from The Arts Council

*but thy life will I give unto thee for a prey
in all places whither thou goest.*

—Jeremiah, 45:5, *King James Bible*

For my parents

And in fond memory of Aedan O'Beirne
(6th August, 1915 - 3rd August, 2010)

Acknowledgements

Grateful acknowledgement is due to the editors of the following publications, where some of these poems first appeared, sometimes in a slightly different form:

Cyphers, Poetry Ireland Review, Southword, The Shop, The Stinging Fly, The Stony Thursday Book, Birmingham Poetry Review, Blue Island Review, Mead: The Magazine of Literature and Libations, Nashville Review, Prick of the Spindle and *No, Dear.*

Part of this book was awarded 2nd prize in the 2008 Patrick Kavanagh Awards.

"The Session at Inch" won the English section of the inaugural (2008) Frances Browne Multilingual Poetry Competition.

Part of "Lazarus" was published in a postcard series of West Kerry-based poets by The Dingle Bookshop, 2008.

"Dún Chaoin" was commissioned for the non-narrative documentary of the same name, about the work of the painter Maria Simonds-Gooding, directed by Lanka Haouche Perren (online at vimeo.com/9760086).

Actor Sam Breslin Wright performed "Unrhymed Sonnet", "A Forest" and "No One Would Know" during various instalments of *Emotive Fruition*, curated and directed by Thomas Dooley, The Bowery Poetry Club, New York, 2010-11 (emotivefruition.org).

Thanks to The Arts Council / An Chomhairle Ealaíon for a generous Bursary granted to me in 2006.

Thanks to Kerry County Council for a grant to stay at The Tyrone Guthrie Centre at Annaghmakerrig in June 2007.

I owe much to the late Pearse Hutchinson, the late James Liddy, and to John Liddy: mil gracias, John. Thanks to Thomas Dooley, Laura McCullough, Ed Skoog, and Rachel Zucker for reading the manuscript, and for their valuable comments. Thanks to Breyten Breytenbach, Kimiko Hahn, Marie Howe, Deborah Landau, Sharon Olds, Brenda Shaughnessy, and my friends at The Lillian Vernon Creative Writers' House. Thanks to Cliff Benston, Amanda Calderón, Lizzie Harris, Scott and Katie Morris, Claudia Patricia Rincón, Charif Shanahan, Kayla Rae Whitaker; thanks to Lucía Atencia, Tara Brennan, Brian Lapan, Fergal Slattery, Peter Costello, Mariele Hesper, Rebecca Evanhoe, Wake Mitchell, Prashant Patel, Creed Shepherd, Jeremy Reh Sidener, David Swenson, Jacqueline Victor. Thank you, always, Sorcha Hyland, Sinéad Kavanagh, Justin McCarthy, Niall O'Higgins.

At Salmon, thanks to Jean Kavanagh, to Siobhán Hutson for making this book, and to Jessie Lendennie for giving these poems such a good home.

Thank you, Adrienne.

And to my family: Rebecca, Marc and Ruth, and my parents, for always believing in me, and these poems.

Contents

Dún Chaoin   15

I

Lazarus   19
Doubting Thomas   21
Saint Christopher Carrying the Christ Child   22
On the Belfast Train   24
'I carried your oxygen'   26
'In the underground car park'   27
Sandymount Strand   28
Two Dancers: Flamenco   29
Saint James the Great as a Young Man   31
Buskers on the Madrid Metro   33
The Irish College at Salamanca   35
Waiting for Saint Brendan   37
Listening to 'Inis Oirr'   39
Navigatio   41
Norwegian Cameo   44
The Paradise of Birds   45
Climbing Mount Eagle   46
Sandymount Strand: Vigil   48

II: Digesting a Scorpion

Young Americans   53
Revenant   54
A Forest   55
Not the Nightingale   56
Golem   58
Mentor   59
Malleus Maleficarum   61
The King of the Crickets   63
And You Had Walked on Water   64
For my Brother   66
Russian Dolls   67

To a Predator   69
Did the Others Witness?   71
Apple   72
Cleaner Wrasse   73
Parasitologist   75
One in Four   76
Witch's Spindle   77
Unrhymed Sonnet   79

III

Sandymount Strand   83
No One Would Know   84
Spider   85
Fort Madison   87
Lawrence, Kansas   88
Euclid Avenue   89
On the Subway   91
Intimacy   92
Beginning of Trust   93
Béal Bán: Nocturne   94
Perseus: Aegis   96
Cuas a' Bhodaigh   98
The Session at Inch   99
The Fish Speaks to Saint Brendan   101

Notes   107
About the Author   111

Dún Chaoin

This could almost be a Hill Station
on the way to the Himalayas, when fuchsia
glitters in the hedgerows after rain,
and through the walls, the sky is visible.
Those young mountains at the world's roof
are still growing. But these, grown inward,
are old and thoughtful, with fields up them,
vertical fields, like ladders up the mountain.
The horizon was scanned by weather eyes—
they played the box at eight in the morning
—still on island time—took pride in how

with a click, each stone found its place,
and walked into exile hobnailed, lonely,
single file. Feeding them dilisk, dulse
and carrageen, giving salt to the earth,
their fields look as if the land made them
—had secreted tender, organic forms
to map the sides of Mount Eagle.
Under a roof of timbers out of the Great Blasket,
you trace that mapping. Building out of need
became an art. Between the waves'

breaths, these forms are drawn in sand.
You breathe, watching the island retreat,
become remote in fog, but still figurative:
the form that has been almost inexhaustible.
Each year, to keep the memory of wells alive
—how easy it is to lose a place—
remembering the places of fresh water,
they go back into the island
to pull the brambles off *Tobar an Phuncáin*
and find the water has cress growing in it,
is still rising from its source.

I

Lazarus

One by one, old men take him by both wrists
and are unable to speak, women kiss his palms,
and those that can, murmur: awed,
a little ashamed, as if queuing to the bereaved.
Under the seething copper cauldron
of the Bethany sun, he sits in a nave
of frozen air, as if carved out of meteorite,
the taut air humming.

And all the while, his sisters clutch his shoulders
—forming the triptych—
their tears in the skin of their teeth
as he looks at the mourners
with eyes like the veil torn in the temple
before an empty tabernacle.

And looking, there were some
who would have buried him again
rather than face his recovery.

                    *

Now that he's here
I don't know what to do with him.
At table he touches things,
then withdraws his hand.
As if there are no words yet
and four days in the dark
cannot be shorthand for a lifetime.

Sometimes, I'm allowed to glimpse him
sitting, his back to the wall,
watching a quiet will as it kindles
knits like living bone.
Day after day, it drags his face to the sun:

the oblique, crone winter sun
unpicking the sutures,
dissolving the shrouds that grew over his eyes
all the time that he was dead.

The seepage of slow, grey-black tears
under the skin
has made his face translucent
and unbearable.
He is water seeking its own level.
Where failure is success,
and success is just a word
sealing the truth.
That there was a defeat,
long ago.

He is a shuffle on linoleum at midnight,
a child at my door at four in the morning
still locked in a terrible dream.
Until I listen, he won't let me go on.

Now he leads me to the threshold
of the first death.
He has crafted caverns to get here:
tunnelled up through the strata of years
unknown, unarmed, unsure of a welcome.
He is rich in grief: caryatids of onyx,
bloodstone, arteries of black diamond
like defined, faceted dark;
the spectrum of deep light.

In the second life,
he will teach me how to live.

Doubting Thomas

Resting before going on, he began
to hear music coming from over the hill.
Though he could see the oasis lights
and taste the camphor fires, he couldn't
imagine the city of arrival: the breaking
of bread, the host pouring water over his hands,
the awful possibility of welcome. Maybe
he did the hardest thing. And found
arriving wasn't what he'd imagined:
a candle flaring in the shocked heart.
Quiet. Undeniable. Or maybe he turned
away one mile from Kerala and went back
all the way he came, to the forest of pillars
in the desert, where love would never find him.

Saint Christopher Carrying
the Christ Child

(After Hieronymus Bosch)

It begins in endurance—and in the marks of endurance—
scored round his dour mouth,
and fugitive eyes
that always see what is behind him:
his house a plague ditch; the black flag
raised over a town put to the crossbow.

He has walked so far
to reach this moment,
it has come too quietly to recognise.
Just a boy, after all,
who asked to be carried
across a river:

blond child
solemn on his shoulder
like a rider in a chariot,
the first two fingers and thumb
of the right hand raised like a play pistol, in blessing.

Walking such a long way
—in search of the moment
where the migratory bird
rests as it flies, into its own flying—
he forgot what he was looking for;
forgot he was looking.

Now the man who carried
whole families begins to understand
what the child weighs
in the scale of things.

After the river, they go on together:
the boy piggy-back,
seeing past the horizons,
the man who gave his soul
to devils and kings

recovering it, mulling it
over. Strange, the way
the search for a true master
leads to the child.

On the Belfast Train

The man pushing the trolley
is my age, wears a stud earring,
and calls me *sir* with a bearing
that has more equanimity
and pride than ever seen south.

Then I catch myself,
thinking of men old
at twenty-eight
watchful, mortgaged
by what they have seen.

*

In the dining car, the cleaning lady
sits in the sun, her white hair,
lemon blouse, the floury folds
of her arms drinking light.
"Oh, I told him, I tell ye.
You can be sure."

"A coffee, please."
"That'll be a pound, buddy."
And when I tender exact change:
"dead-on, fella," the barman replies
relishing directness. But his retina
wanders off, evading interrogation.

*

Across the aisle, a woman
in her forties holds a boy close.
He is yellow-blond,
laughing as she raises him,
smiling, to her eyes.

She holds him like a chalice.
Maybe he is more precious
for coming late.
The boy laughs.
He isn't surprised
to be loved.

I carried your oxygen

and you walked beside me
through the lobby
commenting on the decor
when you needed
to stop
for breath

your hand wren-light
and steady, linking me
through the summer people
with their pints:
polite, not seeing, and oblivious.
I thought I saw you smile
seeing it all equal.

By the ocean of breath
—twice: I remember—
I carried your oxygen.
It was heavy—
a bleak alloy.
Steel.

In Memoriam Edwina Hamill
27th April, 1950 - 12th August, 2000

'In the underground car park'

—*For Katie Armstrong*

In the underground car park
of the mortuary chapel
the brothers in their black suits
are gathering round.
Narcotic fumes hang in the air.
Car doors slam. The coffin slips in.

"I suppose they'll go slowly,"
somebody says.

They'll go slowly through Dublin
until they reach the road to the west
then they'll go like the clappers
to Sligo
through the streaming rain
following their mother home.

Sandymount Strand

Grey sand. Pearl light. Two seagulls wade by the tide marker.
The flock bearing down on you is a flight of white wings,
or a school airborne: moving as one, separating as one around you.
Ochre desert. Wasteland of peace and pearl light.
The red Poolbeg is mute on its whitewashed promontory.
The Bailey, through the cloud massing on the horizon,
glows like a candle in a glass.
Or a window that sees you.

Two Dancers: Flamenco

Before, she sat straight-backed,
her hands clasped
like birds before migration.
Now, with her eyes
and hammering palms
she is forging a scimitar.

A surge within the spine; hot rain;
a slow roll of fire;
lips muttering an invocation
on the edge of the precipice.
And she is not herself
in the final coming-to-rest:

standing with one arm outstretched
and a face pale as bone,
she is Judith, smiling the cruel
inscrutable smile of victory,
throwing us a challenge.
One we are about to accept.

*

Out of stillness, a gesture.
Hand, strong wrist;
fingers spinning air.
Then: passes, feints, preliminaries
—like the wing-struts of a learning bird—
begin to build.

Calmly, the *cantaor* drops one word,
Now, into the kerosene silence,
and suddenly the world is thick with eyes:
a hundred hissing jets of black flame.
It is the dead, keeping vigil.
Their dancer is about to make the journey.

At the front of the stage, he straightens
like a cobra—or a victim
transfixed by the event horizon,
looking for a way to begin.
A way to cross the divide.

Behind him goes the *jaleo*:
now soft, now insistent; understanding,
cruel-to-be-kind:
"si, eso; si. Eso si. Vamos ya.
Ahora."

The spiral rises another level.
And he rises to it, rapt,
blind before the door
where there was no door.
And in the air there is a veil of sweat
like the sweat on the veil of Veronica.

Saint James the Great as a Young Man

(After Ribera)

I am the imaginary friend
you could never quite bring yourself
to believe in,
grown up to early manhood
without you.
Conceived under the red eye of Vesuvius,
now I live always
five hundred miles from home.

With my beard and eyes of mahogany
I could be a minor Symbolist
watching you over my absinthe
from a table at the edge
of the fin de siècle, a Nihilist
from Petersburg who never took action,
a piece of work titled
Young Man Contemplating a Skull.

I could, at last, be
who I really am:
your unknown, northern friend
of the river, the inlet, and the forest
calmly sipping wine
deep in the old town of the city I love,
watching rain on a Sunday
when all the students have flown.

In the end
I was almost the one
who never left
a hundred hedgerow churches
along the banks of the Miño
to die for a cathedral.
To die, with time,
into a lush, vertical reef of stone.

*

I am the novice
among old hands
tough as rope burn,
the intellectual
among fishermen
with cracked, young smiles
fortified by wild garlic and rough wine.

In the gullies of their wrinkles
I see them passing Petra,
coming into Ethiopia to dancing and welcome;
reaching Kerala on pure doubt
—sandals worn to paper, ankles like holm oaks—
to be scattered, then, on the threshing floors
of their anonymous, local martyrdoms.

They are the desert satchels
for gospel truths
that were not taught at school.
For that alone you will find me among them.
But sometimes my face
disappears into darkness
touching the lips of beautiful ambiguity.

I carry a staff,
finger the salt ridges
of a scallop shell.
My taut, white knuckles
already prefigure the path.
But I don't know
if I will fulfil my pilgrimage.

Buskers on the Madrid Metro

The torn nail on the flattened forefinger
of the fat South American Indian
balladeer barring a chord
on the wide fretboard of a flamenco guitar
as he nods the changes across the carriage
to his thin companion with greased-back hair
and almost-defeated eyes.

They are playing a love song
distilled from the highlands of Sierra Maestra
to the dry, empty railroads
at the end of Patagonia:
a bitter *maté* that warms
the blank hearts on the Metro
a little.

So that a blonde woman—painfully thin—
stands up: quiet, smiling.
The Ecuadorian woman beside her
concentrating on her lap
singing along under her breath
from memory.

                *

Sometimes they are in pairs
—running between the carriages
in Islas Filipinas, Colombia,
Tetuán, Cuzco, Banco de España—
but mostly they work alone.

Like the Peruvian man I saw once:
soft guitar case on his back,
pushing the Andes weave-bag
for contributions aside
along one thigh, as he began to play.

Some kneel, telling of mouths to feed
— "por el amor de Dios…"—
but the singer never excuses or begs.
He simply roots himself in the rush
—standing his own against the lurches—

and begins.
Looking at the face formed
on the anvil
—the strange, pooled generosity
of his eyes—
I thought: he's weathered worse.
The rest is singing.

The Irish College at Salamanca

All day that Sunday
the storks wheeled
above the city.
And I remembered
the herons
of the Shannon.

We left the café terraces
of the Plaza Mayor
—tanned women gesturing
over the sun in glasses of white wine—
for quieter streets,
to search for the memory

of those who had come
down the arcades, for years
in the shade of the sun: pale
from waiting in embassy,
politic among the courtiers,
careful; and hoping.

Past the façades of gold stone
we found the college
—white pollen in the air;
weeds between the flagstones.
We were alone there
with our hope for a past, some connection.

The swallows flew low in the cloister
as, like in the *Rue des Irlandais*
in Paris, and Louvain
we stood a long time,
asking the cure
to a homeless predicament.

By the end,
I deciphered enough to understand
I might not always
ask for permission.
Nobles Yrlandeses.
Words that might still ring true.

Waiting for Saint Brendan

The ride of Paul Revere comes to Sarsfield
down uncertain paths. Turning a long corner
the Connecticut Post road
became the Castleconnell bog road,
but only after too many lives.

An Elementary school was my National School.
I learnt the names of minor presidents:
their history before my own. I learnt inflection
listening to mockery. I never asked:
"an bhfuil cead agam… más é do thoil é?"

I waited for the whites of their eyes
on Bunker Hill, until no order came,
and I was overrun. In the playground,
I was the boy who is not seen:
silent, as he learns he is without a people.

Now, I am looking for lost ground
from a time when learning was listening
as stories laid the marrow of belonging.
There was that time too. But sometimes it seems
learning too late casts doubt on what is true.

A life that drifted apart, like the continents
—the islands of Nunavut—
on the tectonic walkways
between Dublin, Shannon and JFK.
I am still at sea, oarless, waiting for Saint Brendan.
But what could he tell me?

*

You always hold off from making landfall.
Man the tillerless boat
to the mouth of Brandon Creek.
You will get there by night or black dawn.
Know it by the scrape of gravel against the gunnel.
Breathe now. Allow yourself,

thread the needle. Climb to Gallarus
where an upturned coracle is an oratory
built stone by stone, without mortar.
But you now, answer me this: how is it
it doesn't let wind and rain in
and remains open to the elements?

Every day, Brandon waits,
beyond the dead gunwale of your horizon.

Listening to 'Inis Oirr'

They were my people
and I depreciated them like old currency
—shillings of sow, hare and wolfhound—
at the boarding gates of the world
because they were awkward and pale
beside the elegant and the tanned,
or playing it garrulous and askew
as the sten guns and Alsatians watched us:
the last Christmas eve flight from Heathrow

the harried, rearguard exodus out of JFK.
Each return funnelled us
from the moulting December Californian palms
to the grey ice piled on the hard shoulders
of New England. There we would meet
on plastic seats, at the gate for Shannon
know the story at a glance,
and be ashamed.

Going home
—where I no longer had a home—
I looked at my own with eyes
that weren't my own
and seeded contempt
for myself.

*

But now the music is beginning
to say what is forgotten.

Listen. Remember.
Salmon, boar, lapwing:
the ones who have been many things
know the world looks back at us.

Waits for you. Continue your descent.
Outside, beyond the moisture
streaming on the pressurised glass,
old eyes search the dark for you.

Navigatio

—For Unn Hatteland and Axel Sømme

Among them on the quayside
I knew them immediately:
the businessmen with beards of blond stubble
and the round glasses of pastors,
babies in haversacks,
white-haired women with knapsacks
and hiking boots at eighty.

I knew them with the shock
of geography: ten-mile tunnels,
wooden houses a primary red
in pine forests, glimpses of islands,
waking at dawn crossing sea bridges
at the mouth of a fjord.

For a month we entered geography
that was always arcing north
to the orange and green
of aurora borealis over Svalbard,
the white spectrum of the Arctic cathedral
at Tromsø, the dizzying islands
of Lofoten, the artists' colony at Dale

sleeping among the birches
the morning after. Easter snow drifting down
in inland mountains. In the morning,
as we watched the fjord's moods
from the picture window
and the fire at night, you laughed
and said: "this is our TV".

We entered a world
where secrets were guarded
about mushroom grounds,
where moose—hunted by your brother—
stewed with chanterelles.
A world of wool slippers

under-floor heating and wood stoves,
children in survival gear on the way to school,
where they still call silence
for forecasts that need four maps
for a country as long as Europe,
and more independent.

Where *it is not a question of weather*
but the clothes you wear to resist it.
—A diffident, blond and red-haired people
who, when asked directions,
simply brought you.
They invented the cheese slicer,
the paper clip, and the *Telemark*: the fast turn
used by the resistance to attack on ski.

In the wood-lined room in old Bergen
we ate the Arctic Cod
that had come down to spawn,
with a sauce made from its own dogged spleen.
After, we pored over the leather-bound Atlas
as you traced the points
that were remote, self-sufficient farms
high on the fingers of the *Hardanger*
and *Sognefjorden*.

I listened to a loving, half-familiar voice
as you named them: Ulvik, Stavanger,
Bodø in the depopulating north
beyond the circle, where, over breakfast
you watched the sun rise
and set, after fifteen minutes of day,
back into grey: three months' oblique
nether-light living below the horizon.

It was a world where sleek, practical cars
with ski racks entered the opening maws
of ferries, but on board
the crews wore the gumboots and beards
of the ocean-going tradition.
Where even the wooden churches
with abstract dragon prows
were about to slip their moorings.

Near the Blue Stone, the meeting place
like an *Ogham* of polished marble,
words like *strand* and *norsk*
set a resonance humming.
Watching the skateboarders
in baggy jeans around the monument
to the ancestors who were our strangers,
I saw the origin of my name.

Norwegian Cameo

Banking over Haugesund,
an old woman in pinstriped trousers,
white wool fleece and black Reeboks
—slighted over the Sterling
for chocolate—looked up,
and as if 40,000 feet
had opened under her,
the young air hostess stopped.

On the liver-spotted hand,
I saw a ring holding shards
of flint and iron: fragments
—like courage—of a tradition
inlaid in the silver.
Her eyes were the longship,
and they were unself-pitying,
and clear.

The Paradise of Birds

Dicuil wrote:
there are many other islands
which can be reached from the islands to the north
of Britain in a direct voyage
of two days and nights with sails filled
with a continuously favourable wind.
A devout priest told me
that in two summer days and the intervening night
he sailed in a two-benched boat
and entered one of them.

There is another set of islands,
nearly all separated by narrow stretches of water.
In these for nearly a hundred years
hermits sailing from our country,
Ireland, have lived. And just as they were deserted
from the beginning of the world,
so now because of the Northmen pirates
they are emptied of anchorites,
and filled with countless sheep,
and very many diverse kinds of sea birds.

I have never found these islands
mentioned in the authorities.

Climbing Mount Eagle

Brook and hill are like good old friends,
Once drunk, and ten years to wake.

("Once More Climbing Shui-hsi", TAO CHI)

—For Justin McCarthy

Now you live under Mount Eagle
ten years after we found the peninsula
—reading portents in the flight of swallows,
granted permissions, cycling roads like green tunnels
towards how we wanted to be.
Pitching our tent at eleven
on a headland west of Baile na nGall,
watching the unreceding curve of the earth
in the blue-black twilight

an old knot loosened
and suddenly there was no more struggle.
It was as if the country had slipped its moorings
and was navigating into a new time zone:
somewhere uncharted, always half an hour
beyond Greenwich Mean Time. I saw an old
fresh place for the first time, had always known it,
where everything is the same—and changed
in the light of the Deep North midsummer.

*

I was nineteen. A long way to the summer
I came back carrying tiredness at thirty, making
strange. The first evening, we sat by the window
watching the mist come down the mountain,
as if recalling other journeys, other mountains.

The next day I climbed the lanes of fuchsia
—the bees among their red-blue lanterns.
Above the black tarn that absorbed the sun

was a silence that was not human,
and it was welcome. Below the top, I sat
and listened to things that knew nothing of us,
nothing of me. I saw Ventry, Dún Chaoin,
the Blasket like a surfacing whale
with its young of outlying islands
—Beiginis, Tiaracht—but empty,
and stripped of their given names.

Seeing all sides of the peninsula so close
was a revelation, but of what, I couldn't be sure.
At dusk, down on the other side,
a voice whispered: *ten years to wake
from the dead.* Then a woman stopped. "Jump in."
I said my birthplace. Like a ward, I said your name.
"I'm from Finglas. I've lived here for twenty years.
Of course I know Justin."

On the way back, in the space of a mile,
I thought: maybe I could belong
again in my own country.

Sandymount Strand: Vigil

On the edge of the strand
speed walkers pace the narrow tarmac
like a landing strip,
or a holding zone
against emptiness.

Beyond the last line of houses
—television mast, church spires,
silent mountains—
the searchings of lighthouses join
and pass across my face.
Here, the sound of traffic
fades with winter light.

Half a mile out, now, slowly,
the million yellow points
ringing the bay—cranes, suburbs
construction night lights—
are smelted, bleed into a torc.

What god will inhabit it
now that we fill all space with ourselves,
grant no point of entry.
Big tankers stalk the horizon.
The poles loosen,
and the compass drifts past true north.
The path fogs with addiction.

Once, there was a prayer.
Hail to the Guardians
of the Watchtowers.
I mouth it

that by the gold, worked, spiral ends
of Binn Éadair and Dún Laoghaire
she would raise it
and, shaking out her hair,
wear the city again.

I stand, and look towards the dark,
the unmanned lighthouses rotating.

II

Digesting a Scorpion

If a child asked for an egg, would you give him a scorpion?
—from LUKE 11:12

But to enter this non-place is to alter everything in the painting and to render impossible a simple return to normal vision. Of course, we do return and reassume that perspective that seems to "give" us the world, but we do so in a sense of estrangement. [...] The non-place that is the skull has reached out and touched phenomenal reality, infecting it with its own alienation.

—*Renaissance Self-Fashioning*, STEPHEN GREENBLATT

Young Americans

2 a.m. in the bars—their stories start to reflect
me. *Mirror, mirror.* Steal our beauty. After shots
of *Old Crow* he confesses to meth, to incest. She—
the serial killer brushed her family off the road.

They circle with intent, and need protection,
as if they want me to be their father, the good man:
their impossible. Like terrible children wanting
to be good, they tell their stories deadpan

well-versed but blank, and mystified,
like people telling stories at the end of a life.
And we're already old, and still unaware
that the enchantment takes years

to unravel, and show, once the tapestry
comes down, plotted in the weft of the underside,
who wove the fabric, who pulled the strings,
when, and how, but never why.

Share your secrets, they plead. But I will not.
After six stiff drinks I lurch clear,
one of the last left at the party still standing,
but still not free. *You're one of us.*

Revenant

I fled Him, down the arches of the years...
Across the margent of the world I fled.

(*The Hound of Heaven*,
FRANCIS THOMPSON)

In the faces that float in the distressed
smoky gossamer of unremembered dreams,
in the people I meet, you've followed me
across four thousand land-based,
nautical miles.

—Coming up for air in the sleep chamber,
I wake in the dark to a distant train.

A Forest

When I was sixteen, it was my favourite song.
And as I listened, I didn't know
that I, too, was lost in a forest.
For years, the trees had multiplied:
A hundred miles and no perspective
spun from the fingers of a witch.
The witch was a man, the man was a priest,
and the spell began as seeds,
dropped casually, into prepared ground.
From an invasive rhizome
a taproot that extended underground,
the forest grew, snagging so thickly
it allowed only a mile of circular movement a day.

The fairytale of the spell that sleeps the world
is true: the castle where even the flies sleep,
where the cook-about-to-beat-the-apprentice sleeps;
my life slept, my will slept, and the forest grew.
He shrank me, so that I became small:
so small, I was mitochondrion,
energy for someone else's self.

Now that I am out in the open,
like a person walking away from a crash
I trust in distance, and keep going:
glad to have survived into the sunlight
that holds no forest within.
But on certain nights
when I wake, I look back
and see the forest has grown on the horizon.
I still see the darkness during the day
and feel the scream, muffled
deep in the place no one can hear.
Then I turn, and walk on.
All I trust is what belongs
to the forward horizon.

Not The Nightingale

It was the lark, the herald of the morn,
No nightingale.

ROMEO AND JULIET (III, v.)

—For N.W.

Sparrow, swallow, hurt songbird:
I wonder where you are now,
and did you make it through the shadow.
Did you make it through the damage
you told to my shoulder
that night at eighteen, when the world stopped
and it seemed we'd always be
cleaved together
like ribs round a common heart.

The deep night outside time
and me in it with you
made it safe to speak
the things that needed the good dark.
What you said, blank-voiced,
hurt the air.
In a room, and a time, that was ours
for one night only, and an hour of morning

I tried to protect you, but had no ward
against his homunculus
growing in me. When you whispered,
"I want you to be inside me,"
it woke to vigilance,
when it saw
I had loved you from the start.

Our teeth clashed
like living, breathing porcelain,
then, for a second,
I was naked inside you.
But also afraid.
I was already in a relationship
with something
that tolerated no other loves
and breaks the future.

Golem

Nicky—we were,
for the record,
ruled by the template
our labyrinth makers
set in motion
in the living conundrum
of our flesh.

I was his golem:
incomplete material.
And the white word
he laid on my tongue
didn't translate as *truth*.
He was no good rabbi.

"Body of Christ, *Davy*,"
he said under his breath,
every Sunday.

Mentor

You gloried in the keenness of your Kestrel eye,
and in that panoptic I was a shrew,
already reduced inside.
When your shadow moved over the grass,
some strength or instinct drove the others
to their burrows: turned-backs, knots of cover.
But you had me cross-haired from on high,
the altar and the blackboard, performing
"The Windhover".

You used to say:
"Davy, you allow me
to be myself. It's wonderful." As mentalists
make hand movements, you took,
and discarded, everything
you could use.

            After I exposed you,
the Consultant Psychiatrist said you were *low risk*:
with your sleight of hand, hypnotic draught,
you made him woozy, too. But someone said,
a therapist reported you were the most devious
he'd ever met, an actor on so many levels
they disappear in penumbra
of the cloister.

Ten years after you, I watched my therapist
fall asleep once in every session.
An eyelid flicker, and for a heavy
second he would become vacant.
It took a month to call him on it.
Another month, and we started calling it

the sleepy feeling. But never
uncovered its provenance.
It lay for years like an unsolved equation.
It was as if we were in a snow globe
of opium poppies, and you were
slowly shaking the glass.

Malleus Maleficarum

Daemones non operantur nisi per artem *

In old Galicia, when it was the forested
Iberian north-west—there are wolves
still in O Courel's mountain fastness—
about witches, people used to say,
"I don't believe in them, but they exist."
It is dangerous to suspend belief.

Fables are hooks, and so you free
them to go to sea in a sieve,
or travel like smoke from the front side
of your face, to take other forms
in the blind spot behind your head
where they are dark educators.

The women some said were witches
knew this: rich in craft of slitting swine,
wizened, headscarved widows
in black with rickety legs
and stout sticks, a quick malice hand
ready to unleash the mastiffs,

they knew ghost lights in the forest
was the Santa Compaña: processions
of lost souls. And not to answer
a knock on the window after nightfall
if it comes with the calling
of your name. You always waited

for someone to say your name.
The old know the door
is fontanelle, still forming,
and that some witches are men.
(I ken warlock means *lesser conjuror*.)

They stopped their ears to the lure
by whispering, I *don't believe,*
but witches exist. The book says:
"after beguiling the door
they can come and go as they please."

* "Demons do not operate save through trickery."

The King of the Crickets

The boy was looking for his voice.
(The cricket king had it).

("The Mute Boy", FEDERICO GARCÍA LORCA)

I see him sitting,
throned
like the awful thing
in Bosch: not bird-headed,
but insect
5 foot 9 in size
growing with voices
but not speaking
his legs sewing,
a machine
to make music.

(ee-ee-eeh-eee-eeh.)

"What is that screaming?"

The voices come.
Some are tempted by
some magic on the air,
but minions carry most in,
and he eats them.
He eats them head-first,
like children, and doesn't stop
until he is stopped.

But no one can find him.

To find this place (it is no where),
you have to go back
into the throne room
via the stump of silence.
You must enter through the wound
you have already sustained.

And You Had Walked on Water

There hath he lain for ages and will lie...
Until the latter fire shall heat the deep;
Then once by man and angels to be seen,
In roaring he shall rise and on the surface die.

("The Kraken", TENNYSON)

You said: "*God*, you're so formal.
Look at how Marc's dressed.
He comes home from cheffing
and throws on torn jeans with a black suit
jacket from Brown Thomas. *Perfect*."

Then later, at dinner
(you weren't paying—you never paid),
you said: "look at how elegant
Davy is in a suit!"
You made it visible so easily:
the sharp filament of the double bind.

Your complex
shielding was slipping,
the trance wheel of colour
slowing, your disguises grinding
to a halt. The chains had fed out
for miles, clanking in silence
in the Mariana trench, 5000 fathoms down.

Where you'd glided,
now you were beginning to snag
on the lives you had subsumed.
The truth emerged—dripping,
armoured, ancient with feelers
from where it had always been,
just below the surface

and you had walked on water.
I saw you small on the denuded sea floor.
I saw your machinist: little freak
manipulating the gears. You were
not as careful as before,
when you'd moved slower than time-
lapse photography; or the game *Statues*.

For the first time, you rushed, and I saw you.
A month later, I told the truth on you:
and never saw you again.
Or heard the voice of wheedling
power: though hear it still in dreams,
and waking dream, when anyone says,
"Hey, Davy!"

                  I shake it off like sleep.
"That's not my name anymore."

For My Brother

Thirty years will pass before I remember
that moment…

("You Can Have it", PHILIP LEVINE)

I read *brother*
and immediately think of him:
wild, contrary,
secretly caring deeply,
handsome, discreet as a stone
with our secrets,
braver than me.
And so I think,
should he not have been
the elder brother?

Would, then, the things that happened
not have happened
if he'd been the older,
because some warning
would have sounded
when he met the abuser?

Or, maybe, in part, he is these things
because I was the sandbags
so that the breach wouldn't happen
further in, further on down the line.

Russian Dolls

We must throw the entire painting out of perspective
in order to bring into perspective what our usual mode
of perception cannot comprehend.

(*Renaissance Self-Fashioning,* STEPHEN GREENBLATT)

Like an excavationist, the postcolonial
lecturer said to us—hundreds ranged up
the insides of the hive—"look at the shape
under their feet in this masterwork by Holbein."
They stand in ermines, proud, bearded
men of civilisation, a table of sextants,
two globes—compass and meaning—
behind them: ambassadors to the court
of Henry VIII, "which must have been
like the Politburo under Stalin." You
had to whittle yourself, if there was
such a concept then. Treading water,
the sudden cold beneath your chest.
The buffeting.

You have to stand at an angle to see
the skull that was there all along.
Is there a term in art for radical infestation
of the surface meaning?
In life there is no word
for when the floor falls away.

It is strange what comes back to you.
Reading *The Revenger's Tragedy*
my baggage seemed light,
like microfiche, and I believed I was free.
Strange and ominous to remember
things you thought were true—
reality reshaken in the kaleidoscope,
your own body's atoms

collide in the memory accelerator.
It is atomisation, falling apart
as the lies come together,
as the feelings that were blocked
bleed back, you feel you are dying alive,
within yourself, within him,
he within you, lies within truth within lies—

Russian Dolls, coffined,
and inside: you, the
tiniest thing.

To a Predator

By means of this disk the "Sucking-fishes" or "Suckers" attach
themselves to sharks, turtles, ships [...] Being bad swimmers they
allow themselves to be carried about by other animals or vessels
with greater powers of locomotion.

(An Introduction to the Study of Fishes
ALBERT C. L. G. GÜNTHER)

You cut the water for me,
brutal with your snout
that was the whole front side
of your head.

You had gouges
the size of star fish,
whip-lash from giant squid,
and whip marks
from Portuguese Men o' War,
rough trade of dealing with mantas
and moray eels.
Being savagely wounded was glory.

You were efficient
at getting what you wanted;
but so patient,
sensing young prey a mile off
as if tasting the electrical field
of living things.

I thought I was your only one.
But others clung to you
in the blue-darkness
of the water.

Down there, there were no stars;
no phosphorescence.
The nibble of your grooming
made it seem you were the sun.
But all it was, grey, mottled,
was your skin, close up,
and you hidden within it,
grinning.

I found out about your other remora
later: the small ones flying near your mouth
the others near your underside.
You held us
in separate chambers
of water.

Years later, I followed decisive girlfriends
at shoal work of parties.
I didn't swim for myself.
Where did I learn that tendency?
I asked myself.

Did the Others Witness?

"We didn't"—"see"—"I mean"—"the water was murky"—
"we didn't"—"*know*"—"that is to say"—"we were"
—"swimming"—"nearby"—"I suppose"—
"but"—"the pilot fish"—"they were friends"
—"with him, you know"—"those pilot fish!"—
"they were swimming ahead"—"scouting"—"they say"
—"that rumour"—"they have a special"—"relationship"—
"with Great Whites"—"but we didn't"—"see"—"such shoals"
—"couldn't see much"—"saw nothing, in fact"—"shoaling

the blue haze"—"and the wrasses"—"and their cleaning stations"—
"then—when the blue fin come"—"they obscure everything"
—"oh,"—"had my suspicions"—"couldn't be proved,
though"—"we"—"of course, I"—"remember"—"vaguely"—
"I said to you at the time"—"you wouldn't"—"listen"—
"couldn't disabuse you"—"of it"—"but nothing can be proven"—
"I stopped you"—"you seemed"—tousled"—"flushed"—
"flustered"—"I looked you in the eye"—"as if looking for"—
"evidence"—"maybe"—"I mean, I sometimes thought"—"he was"

—"a rough educator"—"But"—"procedures"—"put in place"—
"all reasonable"—"measures, you know"—"the wrasses"—
"were attending the groupers"—queuing up"—"amongst the kelp"
—"the hammerheads were approaching"—"such a blue haze"
—"couldn't really know"—"what was happening"—
"anyway, a rogue element"—"how could I?"—
—"we were schooling"—"not as if you could"—
"hold us responsible"—"the seaweed forest"
—"made it hard to see"—

Apple

Juice ran down
your chin as you ate,
looking at me nonstop
during the act:
your eyes empty
except for the need to take
everything, and a veiled
calculation.

I was passive, left my body.
(I still leave like that.)
My body fought
and remained flaccid.

You always ate the whole apple
core and all: your metaphor
for swallowing the bitter
with the sweet. Sometimes
I catch myself biting
an apple seed, the firm
inner white in a bitter
brown sheath, and shudder

at having learnt
everything from you.

Cleaner Wrasse

At a time when young wrasses
nibble and groom
—elaborate filaments of first touch
and the algae of nest-building—
right at the time when we start
to secrete futures,
an adult of another species
came to the cleaning station.

Was he tench, or flounder?
Bottom feeder for certain,
but unfamiliar
among our usual clientele.
There were sharp reef fragments
so deeply embedded,
they grew in the lateral side
of his secret, ugly face.

He came and insinuated—
bubbles from his mouth
enclosed me—if I took care
of his skin and gills,
he would protect me:
unconditional, in exchange
for conditional things:
access to my mouth
and small, perfect breath slits.

He would praise me
if I fed on his dead
tissue: the edges
of what billowed on the other side
of his face, cuts
like the thick lips
of my own species.

As I cleaned,
I was induced further in.
I began to travel him,
a reef castle.
I didn't see that other young
were part of the walls
grown there
behind white bars of cartilage.

They had been preserved
at the juvenile stage:
when we do not yet know
who we are.
I didn't know the pus paths
went all the way to his interior:
to the small, two-chambered heart.

Now there is nothing left.
The one who hid among us,
pretending to be Doctor Fish
of consolation, has gone.
And I am still travelling him,
arrested as if enchanted.

They say we sleep in crevices
between rocks or corals,
covered in a slime layer we secrete at dusk.
They say in the morning, the remains
can be seen floating on the surface.

Parasitologist

Parasites are one of the most undiagnosed
health challenges (in fact, they're all around us)

and are very hard to detect.
Frankly, most professionals aren't trained

to look for them, or even know the symptoms.
Most people can't even begin to imagine

the many kinds of bizarre and devastating effects
they can have on the hosts they colonise.

Scientists who study parasites are amazed
at their resourcefulness.

There seems to be no limit
to how easily they can jump from host to host,

and how they complicate their life cycles
to ensure their survival.

They can mimic their hosts to go undetected,
and slip past normal defenses.

Then they fool their host
into providing protection.

One in Four

It has happened to a quarter of us
(*us?* Is that a community?)
twenty five out of every one hundred
hung, hearts, spleen, and lungs
drawn, and everything is quartered,
memory split, hemisphered
like a dangerous rebel carcassed
and dispatched to the corners of the realm,
the Elizabethan, Cromwellian, Rome-subjugated
territory, so that no one will ever forget

or remember
twenty-five percent of this population
has been butchered.

The memories start to live back
through the limbic system
fragments of stained touch,
the flashbacks come
in the arms of real love.

Until it can be said,
until I can say, *me too*,
the crime will continue.
I join my voice to the silent chorus
to hold space for those who can't speak yet.
I speak, and I hold.
Hold the line.

Witch's Spindle

I find it hard to fathom
the years it takes to travel
up into the speech range.

Last look at the false charts
the pilot gave
before I give them to the fire.

There is a beginning of love
jeweled in her eyes. Am I tiny
or full size?

I watched friends
on the other side of love
and wondered, how is love done?

This is mapping
what it is when you never want
to be found.

I was someone's instrument
put me in the unnatural
way for the young of not wanting

my hair to shine or take light
in: not wanting glorious
or beautiful. "Shame on your body,"

he whispered. "Privacy is exquisite.
Stay unpublished. I am your best reader,
like *Narziss*. You are my *Gold-*

Mund, Davy."
In this twining,
you can be lost for years

and great straw work gets done
in the room at the top of the tower
(it exists between the hours of the numeral clock)

where the spindle is. The door to the room
only appears when the witch wants,
when the finger is to be pricked

and the sleep begins. In my country
the male witches rule always
the under-territories of silence.

There was a beauty
to the forests of hunted song birds
around the castle

like a virginity bled white.
The landscape slept, naïve
around me as the witches

went about their rituals, as if circling
a finger on the altar, twining it
more and more nerveless.

Unrhymed Sonnet

To beguile the time,
Look like the time…

MACBETH (I, v.)

He was in my dream last night. I won't say *again*.
It has been some time. But enough to say,
last night he was in my dream, to any of four friends
and they know how it eclipses the days.

He was there in the dream: silent, posturing,
obscene, making me lie. Like a bramble
he spread speculative feelers into my life
and waited, patient, invisible in plain sight.

But follow it down the years, down twenty years,
all the way to the root. Then tell the loves I lost
(their gentle voices shake me out of the dreams),
tell them why I needed sanctuary

at twenty nine. Explain why I woke afraid.
But not off course, now. Not ever again.

III

Sandymount Strand

Nothing happens here.
A man walks his dog
between rivers that carve out
temporary, treacherous deltas.
The sand sucks at your boots
as you stand for a long time

looking at the lights of the ships
passing the shelf of the South Wall.
The bay's old noose around you.
And yet, the noise of history
grows mute the further out you go.
You come here because once

too much happened.
And even now
a reverberation can sweep
everything out in the undertow
flowing to emptiness
down the levels of emptiness

where gulls mock in immense space
—*ask the right question!*—
and shelter where there is no shelter
in flocks that run
along the tide rivers
rivering out to sea.

In a blue-grey light
a couple walks towards Booterstown,
and the spires of Dún Laoghaire
unreal behind rain:
restored by distance
to figures in a landscape.

No One Would Know

—For Jude

Apart from a distant, reflective cast of light
in your grey-green eyes, certain moments
on days that turn them greyer—more distant
than fingers of rain a mile out on a sea horizon—
no one would know to look at you
that you've fought monsters, and the mothers
and fathers of monsters, down in the dark
tunnels under the lake with no Beowulf sword,
that you've come through slaughter, incurred
heavy losses to live in the light again.
Even if they never gave you the ticker tape,
the parade, welcome to the world, my friend.
All I ask is that you take my hand
when it's my turn to come through.

Spider

O honey-bees,
Come build in the empty house of the stare.

("Meditations in Time of Civil War", W.B. YEATS)

I've just seen her again.
Maybe she has come to live
among the blank and filled
diaries—sometimes pages
to fill a fool's cap—
stacked at the back
of the cheap chipboard desk
that has no view.

I saw her last night, flying
above the notebook.
After some time, she rested
on the wall, dwelling in the wide
field of her own white page.
Watching the tiny, gold,
motionless scarab
—she seemed to sleep—

I remembered the story
of how Vishnu rests
between ages of creation
and I was breathed down
to a slowness where it seemed
perfected: this—just being here.
Something else has come
into the I's compound, its white

cuboid compression.
I know if one is the guest,
the other's the host.
But she has come to build
among the pages.
I can feel the stitch
moving—threading, dissolving—
like it was in my own body.

Fort Madison

Stepping off the train for the smoke break,
as Mennonite families clambered down
and a teenaged girl in a white bonnet, big glasses
and jeans ran off up the platform to stretch her legs,
a young black guy in a hoodie checking his smart phone
looked at me and shook his head: "shoot, man, no
coverage," and I thought of jazzmen, always
travelling back to Union Station, always Kansas City.

Just then, a hunched Amish man with a straw boater,
black shirt and black trousers
and a long, black, white-streaked Swedish beard
met my eye in the glow of his roll-your-own,
as if to say: we are not so strange; we are not strangers.
What the smell of the moment was,
whether of pig swill, corn fertiliser
or chilled peach skin, I couldn't tell.

There had been a red light winking,
a barge or a train,
as we crossed a wide, dark body of water
moving slowly between silty, clayey banks
fringed with young-seeming winter trees
—names like *cottonwood*, names out of books—
until I realised it was the Mississippi we were crossing
from Illinois into Iowa, in a strange place.

As they called the all aboard
I glimpsed the Formica and linoleum
of the empty, small-scale waiting room,
the chairs upholstered lime and lapis-blue,
the Station Master's rooms warm in the dark,
and thought I saw *Ti Jean*—Jack Kerouac,
outsider still in love with America
still waiting for his train.

Lawrence, Kansas

—For Sorcha Hyland

While you're in the kitchen with Osiris,
Melissa—long-black-haired, and slightly in earnest
—crosses the street with Eve, her two-year-old,
to ask the lend of a bike to go and vote
here, the only blue county in Kansas.
Eve explores red leaves under the porch swing,
listens to Indian Summer crickets
as I ask Jeremy about the flag's absence.

He carries it up from the basement, tied
on a wooden pole tipped by a bronze eagle.
And, as he hoists it, he says, "*Old Glory*"
—that Kansan touch in his inflection:
the way, here, they still say "Missoura"—
and watches as it begins to flap in a new wind.

(4th November, 2008)

Euclid Avenue

The end of thinking is hard to imagine.
—Hardest thing to decouple the carriages.
I know too little of balance, or symmetry,
and when the train of thought
finally comes into station, it wasn't that car at all
but the next one that was the mother of worry.
What would I do without my boxcars
of terrible geometry?

Connection is available for PATH

Maybe at Atlantic we'll all interchange,
or gather at the river for the Franklin Ave. shuttle
to Euclid Avenue.
"If I take the F, can I reach Myrtle?
Will you grant me your peace at Dekalb?"

By night, I am summoned, textually, by your needs.
Ever practical in daylight, you say: "Myrtle?
you'll have to go all the way into Manhattan
and take the L, unless you want to try the G,
the cross-town local, a time-consuming prospect."
Then, the theorist in you: "you see,
until recently Brooklyn wasn't a destination."

In the dream, though, you take me literally,
standing like an oracle in the door of the B;
I'm on the same platform, F, effigy,
and though not even half an alphabet away,
there's no chance to explain.

In this city
there's no real beauty contest for trees:
which bird flies higher, the eagle or the wren,
over the Beech Walk, or the linden trees of Berlin.
Who is learning to walk slow?
Or happy with being invisible?

Maybe the old man in Donegal tweed
on the platform bench
clear-eyed, with still hands
among these anxious souls
checking their texts, blackberrying,
is almost an angel. For a moment
he could be my grandfather.

These faces on the bough:
there, and then gone.
Faces within the surfaces of the river,
faces beneath convexities of rain
travelling together, and then away,
like the yellow windows of parallel trains
diverging beneath Alphabet City,
the angles and panes
of dis-assembling isosceles triangles.

Connection is available

The last thing you say is:
"who lives at Euclid Avenue?"
and have gone before I can answer.
I imagine a place of calm symmetry
and placid solution, found through axiom, rule and proof,
though in the waking and the dream,
I've never been to Euclid Avenue.

On the Subway

Among the people nodding like Narcissus
—deep in their own devices,
but deaf to other modulations—
a salve: near midnight
a tall black working man
in big working man's boots
puts his hand on the rail by my head
—pink convex nails,
calloused hand,
nearly a barber's touch—
and sings a few bars
of something quiet, and private
—for himself.

Intimacy

Seven years ago
in a grotty hostel in Fez,
the smell of old tom cat
territorial spray in the room,
you asked me to come with you
down the hall to the common bathroom.
Then, when we were there,
you didn't trust the toilet seat
and asked me to lift you. I lifted you,
sustaining you while you pissed,
laughing, shy, loving me.
It's almost as if nothing
has been the same, since.

Beginning of Trust

I've forgotten for how long now
I have fallen asleep
knowing you'll be there tomorrow.
It influences even the way I breathe
and rest into dreams.

And I'm here,
listening to you breathe beside me
in the night light:
I'm here, looking at you,
amazed at your trust
in sleep, in love, in me.

I want to wake you
and tell you what has happened.

Béal Bán: Nocturne

(21st June, 2007)

The breeze comes almost cold, now:
a hot hint of silage in it; tentative calling of sheep,
distant breakers against Baile Dháith Head
even on the calmest day.
Starlings rush low over stone walls
as if hurrying against the light, poised
at ten o'clock like a muted evening in winter:
something in slow equilibrium.

And I'm still looking towards Brandon,
from a different angle.
It seems a long time since I stood at the sink
watching the mountain generate weather
like a god, those days in November he drew the veil,
like Mount Fuji, all the way to the ground:
cattle calling through a fine salt mist,
as if we were at sea.

From my desk I watched the sea darken.
Another squall coming. As horizontal rain hit the window
I bent to the page, learning to write more than *I*
and you entered my poems.
The wind woke us in the beginning.
We would huddle together, or go to the window;
but night after night the house stood its ground.
It knew Feothanach means wind.

That February, two swans appeared in the breakwater.
They stayed a week, fanning their wings in the surf
on evenings of clean red sunsets,
wet black stones laid out like a chessboard.
I took them as a sign: in their slight disorientation
like blow-ins getting their bearings;
that they didn't belong, but that together,
any place they were together, made sense.

Now, I seem to be returning to nights on Sandymount Strand
when it seemed easier to see with no one to share it;
except, I'm here now, where night comes last:
south-south-west and not getting a bearing,
watching the first lights glitter across the bay
reflecting through glass where Brandon is veiled;
not even a mirage clarifying out of the distance
to see: yellow moon, reflecting on white strand.

Perseus: Aegis

But he managed to glimpse
Her dread form reflected in the polished bronze
Of a circular shield strapped to his left arm.

Metamorphoses, OVID
(Translated by Stanley Lombardo)

Around its rim is etched the dead gods
—like lids, opening around what
the goddess gave to be my eyes
even as I went forward—crabwise—
into the place that eats light.
Where no human had been.

She said: *when you go to the sulphur gates,*
better go armed with something equal
to it. And hope that angels stand
at the unassuageable gap
like the terrible, raging, prayed-for
protectors of the Dharma.

As the shield-arm splinters
the mirror-shield distributes the blow:
shivering, holding steady,
holding its own at the eye
of the cyclone—witnessing,
even as I am turned to stone.

The shield still exists—tarnished, beaten
greened silver, like a sapling
opened by lightning,
the city of the four directions
engraved in the malachite,
a mandala continuing underground.

Ever since, I sift poisoned soil
for the dulled glint of adamant:
the sudden shock of its edge. The centre
is still gouged with the original story:
the pupils contract, see me coming.
Wait for me.

Follow the map given by fear.
Now, child.

Cuas a' Bhodaigh

Not many find their way here.
After the islands, riding luminous
and unreachable in the Sound,
and the Three Sisters, dreaming,
this is the end of the road.

But as you drove here
through the sedge grass
and reeds of Feothanach
—*croí na teanga*—
you were preparing yourself for Cuas:

shedding other landscapes
for the simplicity of the bridge
over a stream
that runs into the sea
at the end of a world

the cobbled slipway, a few boats
in the natural harbour
—just a gash in black cliffs,
afterthoughts of Mount Brandon—
the frightening simplicity that says

the road ends here.
If you want to continue,
either navigate or climb.
There is nowhere else to go.
A breeze ripples the water

as if Brendan had just left harbour.
And you walk back from the pier
the way you would after seeing off a friend,
back to the only life you have
hesitant, but resolved.

The Session at Inch

—For Justin McCarthy and Niall O'Higgins

As the third reel was flung wide
and the first shiver began to run over the skin
Tom stood and started dancing
beside his bar stool.
They murmured, as if at taboo.
But when the musicians saw his eyes
brooding behind their lids
his listening—like a mirror—
began to concentrate the fire.

But each time they nodded
the chord-change
to bring it to an end
he kept dancing:
neat, never-learnt steps
goading, daring them on.
Roars of *go on!* began coming, then,
to the unknown English dancer

who answered them—lips tight,
sweating—with glints of gold in the firelight
from the necklace of small things
he had found along the way.
The jangle extended, into the atonal,
like the bells of steppe horses;
or a dancer of the tundra
circumscribing himself within a circle
tight as the skin on a seal drum

in which he was, over and over,
defining, and freeing space.
The bow of a fiddle angled high
catching the light,

until each instrument raised, and held it.
Then we were all in the one circle:
at one end of the house
an open fire,
the front door open to the sea.

The Fish Speaks to Saint Brendan

When a shark, taken on the hook, is drawn out of the water
the sucking-fish leaves it instantly, and is capable of much speed
in swimming on its own account.

(A *Guide to the Study of Fishes,* DAVID STARR JORDAN)

You were not a war boat
or an orca
though seal-greasy and almost alive
to my sucker's touch.
Your people want to know
did we help or hinder
when we swam with your boat.
In terms of our traditions
of hospitality, a gentle parasitism,
neither, I'd say. We are fish
of necessary delay.

I know you yourself stopped
for a spot of lunch
around Iceland, on the whale's back.
What did she say
when you lit a fire under her blow hole?
Dipping back in,
she didn't tolerate you
and your crew.

And so, you were almost the same
strange fish as me,
going in for the kind of freedom
that's defined by lack

of oars. Swum upside down
it washes back as *saor*: cheap,
or free, in the current sense;
good man in Old Irish:
autonomous, artificer

out of the tradition
of going on a sea penance,
the white martyrdom:
shipping oars and going Christ knows
where, out of the original peninsula
of clouds back-lit with sunlight,
shadows moving fast over the green hide
of Brandon
before it got your name.

You left long before the lookouts
on the Armada sighted the mountain
and the Santa María de la Rosa
entered Blasket Sound
—ship's boy the only survivor—
and the Spanish woman, *nobile*, washed up
in Dún Chaoin. They wondered at the dress of tulle,
drifting with a pulse
like their own greenish-black dulse.

If my name is *delay*,
then you were always one of us
on a terminally sideways
north Atlantic drift.
You shipped oars
via the Viking Gyre
to Greenland
and let the current
take you.

And this is the freedom of a fish
taken for parasite.
You see, I swim well on my own
and know my real size.
Neither Priapus nor Poseidon,
demi-god of no ocean,
I'm a strange one, entirely,
in that of my genus,
I'm mainly north Atlantic

though I've washed up
on the Durban coast at times.
Cape of Needles,
the Cape of Good Hope:
it depended entirely
on who I was riding.

I've been attached to secretary fish, civil servants
who shone at night with their own phosphorescence
in chosen watering holes;
Third Secretaries to mammalians
minor diplomats to tyrants,
they submerged their scales
and drowned their gills
garbled in muted surface colours;

I've been a friend to drinkers, users
and the abused, warriors,
bottom feeders, prisoners
who wrote with quill cartilage
cut from their own breathing apparatus,
slack sailors who jumped ship
into 10 year ruts
that were velvet, and lotus,
friends who went into the black
abyssal plain of Challenger Deep
and never came back—

I will hold to them
like a leaf boat of bullock leather
that proved itself worthy,
good and salt-caulked
whelk-cankered, cantankerous
and everything else they say about me.

Because the boat out of Cuas
made the journey—
and came back none the wiser,
you might say.
But it came back, oars shipped.
That is remora.

Notes

Dún Chaoin: the Great Blasket Island was the home of an entirely Gaelic-speaking community that included writers Peig Sayers, Tomás Ó Criomhthain and Muiris Ó Súilleabháin. "Tobar an Phuncáin": "Well of the Yank". The island was abandoned in 1953 due to old age and emigration. The islanders settled mainly in Dún Chaoin (Dunquin), the closest mainland village, or emigrated to Springfield, Massachusetts, where they were initially noted for walking single file. The island's paths are usually too narrow to do otherwise.

Doubting Thomas: Thomas the Apostle is said to have brought Christianity to India.

Sandymount Strand: The Bailey and Poolbeg are lighthouses in Dublin Bay.

Two Dancers: Flamenco: in the Bible, Judith beheads the Assyrian general Holofernes. "Cantaor": singer. "Jaleo" is the supportive back-talk integral to Flamenco. The Spanish translates as "Yes, that's it; yes. Let's go. Now". In apocryphal tradition, Saint Veronica wiped Christ's face with her veil on his way to the cross. The "veronica" is a bull-fighting pass where the matador "wipes" the bull's face with the cape.

Saint James the Great as a Young Man: Saint James the Great is the patron saint of Spain. In local tradition, after his martyrdom by Herod, the saint's remains were brought by angels, via a stone boat, to the site of Santiago de Compostela cathedral: the third-most important place of medieval Christian pilgrimage after Jerusalem and Rome. The painting "Santiago el Menor" (Saint James the Less") hangs in the Prado among a series of portraits of the Apostles for which Ribera used Neapolitan fishermen as models. The river Miño flows from Lugo, in Galicia, into Portugal.

Buskers on the Madrid Metro: Sierra Maestra is a mountain range in southeastern Cuba with a long revolutionary history. "Por el amor de Dios": "for God's sake".

The Irish College at Salamanca and Waiting for Saint Brendan: from the 16th - 18th centuries, during the Penal Laws, Catholic services could only be conducted in private. Catholics were barred from military service and public office, thus ushering in a Protestant Ascendancy, and the end of the native Gaelic Order. Irish

Colleges were set up throughout continental Europe for the education of Irish priests and lay Catholics. "Nobles Yrlandeses": the old Spanish spelling for "Noble Irish".The Irish exiles hoped for Spanish and French military intervention in Ireland. Patrick Sarsfield was a Jacobite leader who went into exile with his army in 1691 after the Treaty of Limerick, in what has become known as "The Flight of the Wild Geese". "An bhfuil cead agam dul go dtí an leithreas más é do thoil é?" is the rote question by which National school children ask: "may I please go to the toilet?" Gallarus Oratory is an early Christian church, reminiscent of an upturned boat, located on the Dingle Peninsula south of Mount Brandon, the Gaelic for which, "Cnoc Bréanainn", translates as "Brendan's hill".

Listening to 'Inis Oirr': 'Inis Oirr' is a traditional slow air. Inis Oirr / Inisheer is the smallest Aran Island.

Navigatio: refers to the "Navigatio sancti Brendani abbatis", the Latin text about St. Brendan the Navigator's journey to the western "Isle of the Blessed", circa 512 AD. Norway claimed Johan Vaaler as the inventor of the paper clip. During the Nazi occupation, Norwegians wore it on their lapels as a sign of resistance. McLoghlin is the anglicisation of Mac Lochlainn, son of Lochlann "of the lakes", "Lochlannach" meaning Scandinavian, or Viking, thus: "son of the Viking".

The Paradise of Birds: the poem's language is from James J.Tierney's translation of Dicuil's *Liber De Mensura Orbis* (The Dublin Institute For Advanced Studies, 1967), pp. 75- 77. In *The Brendan Voyage,*Tim Severin argues that the islands Dicuil mentions are the Faroe Islands, and argues convincingly for the stepping-stone route taken by Brendan via Scotland, The Faroes and Iceland. He did this by reaching Newfoundland from Ireland in a leather boat of period-specific design.

Climbing Mount Eagle: The epigraph is from "Views of the South", by Tao Chi (China, 17th Century, tr. by Roderick Whitfield, in Anne Bancroft's *Zen: Direct Pointing to Reality,*Thames & Hudson, 1979). Except for Finglas (traditionally, a working class suburb of Dublin), the places named are in West Kerry. Ireland was GMT minus 25 minutes until 1916.

Sandymount Strand: Vigil: torcs are open-ended neck rings, found in European Iron Age cultures, made from bronze or gold. Binn Éadair (Howth) and Dún Laoghaire are at opposite ends of Dublin Bay.

Malleus Maleficarum (1486) was the treatise on identifying witches, by the inquisitor Heinrich Kramer.

The King of the Crickets: the quote from Lorca is the author's own translation.

Golem: a mud or clay servant in Jewish folklore animated either by a rabbi's placing the Hebrew word for life in its mouth, or by his writing the word *truth* on its forehead.

Parasitologist: the text of this poem is from the following website: www.therealessentials.com/parasites.html. Permission has been sought.

One in Four: the Irish charity "One in Four" is at the forefront of advocating for the rights of those who have suffered sexual violence.

Béal Bán: Nocturne: the Gaelic name of this West Kerry beach translates as "white mouth". "Feothanach" is the Gaelic for "windy place".

Perseus: Aegis: in Tibetan Buddhism, the *Dharmapalas* ("Defenders of Buddhism") are depicted in ferocious, wrathful form, and are imagined as engaged in constant warfare against evil.

Cuas a'Bhodaigh (Brandon Creek) is the cove at the foot of Mount Brandon from which Brendan is said to have set out on his journey. "Croí na teanga" translates as "heart of the language", and refers to West Kerry's Gaeltacht / Irish-speaking status.

To a Predator and The Fish Speaks to Saint Brendan: Remoras are thin, quite dark fish, ranging from a few inches to over three feet long, common to warmer seas. Their first dorsal fin is a modified suction disc with which they fasten to whales, sailfishes, turtles, and sharks. The family name, *Echeneidae*, comes from the Greek, "echein": to hold, "naus": a ship. In Latin remora means "a stop, a delay, hindrance, obstruction"; among the remora's common names, along with suckerfish and shark sucker, is ship-holder. Pliny the Elder made the first literary reference to this belief in his *Historia Naturalis*, where the remora is blamed for Mark Antony's defeat at the Battle of Actium. When a shark finds food, the remora detaches itself to eat the scraps. But apart from finding its own prey—if it is conveniently close—remoras feed on shark ectoparasites. The relationship is symbiotic: the remora gains transport and food, while the shark is relieved of parasites. Because of the shape of its jaws, its coloration, and the sucker's appearance, remoras sometimes appear to be swimming upside-down. This probably led to the older common name reversus. (Adapted from *The Natural History of Sharks* by T.H. Lineaweaver and R.H. Backus (Lyons & Buford, 1984), "Remora" in *Encyclopaedia Britannica* and *Webster's Dictionary*.)

DAVID MCLOGHLIN was born in Dublin in 1972, and studied at University College Dublin, where he was awarded First-class honours for his Master's thesis on the Spanish poet Luis Cernuda. He also holds an MFA in Creative Writing from New York University, where he was an editor of *Washington Square* review, and received a fellowship to teach creative writing to patients at Goldwater Hospital. His poems have appeared in literary journals such as *Poetry Ireland Review*, *Cyphers*, and *The Stinging Fly*. He received an Arts Council Bursary in 2006, was awarded 2nd prize in the 2008 Patrick Kavanagh Awards, and most recently was the Howard Nemerov Scholar at the 2011 Sewanee Writers' Conference. He currently lives in New York. www.davidmcloghlin.com